DEDICATION:

To all the awesomely autistic
adults, finding their way through
life in a hostile world. I see you,
you're doing a great job.

contents

HOW TO USE THIS WORKBOOK

If you are reading this, chances are you are currently experiencing some degree of an identity crisis about your entire life, stemming from the creeping realisation that... gasp!... you might be autistic.

I totally get it - I've been there myself - and I understand it can be a very confronting and emotional time. You may find yourself revisiting your past and having to re-evaluate all your beliefs about who you are and who you thought you were.

This is entirely normal.

Trust me that your identity is intact and you will come out of this with a deeper understanding of who you really are, and hopefully a little more compassion for yourself.

And that's really the point of this book.

This is a workbook of self-discovery, it is intended to be written in, scribbled on, referred to, and held late at night while you're sobbing about small things that happened 30 years ago that suddenly just *make sense* now (I would appreciate feedback on whether your tears make the ink run).

Although I've primarily aimed this at adults, it could certainly be used by (older) teens too.

WHO ARE YOU ANYWAY? YO SAMDY WHAT?

For those of you who don't know me already (nice to meet you by the way!), my name is Sam and I run the YouTube channel "Yo Samdy Sam" where I make videos about autism and the neurodivergent experience.

I was diagnosed as autistic at the age of 33, after a lifetime of mental anguish and a persistent feeling that I wasn't quite "right".

The years surrounding my diagnosis were a time of great reflection and transformation, and ultimately I came out of it with so much more confidence and trust in myself.

I was an awesome autistic, not a broken neurotypical.

Now I make videos and put them on the internet and call it a "job".

For those who find it hard to interpret tone, especially through the written word, please know that I write this workbook with love, silliness, absurdity, and just a pinch of sarcasm scattered throughout.

But it doesn't really matter who I am, because this workbook is about you. It's the book I wish I had before - and after - I was diagnosed.

WHY DO I NEED A WORKBOOK? ISN'T A DIAGNOSIS ENOUGH?

Of course the person selling the workbook is going to tell you that you need it, but since you've probably already bought it, I'll try to reassure you that you've done the right thing.

This book is not intended as a replacement for an autism diagnosis or psychological treatment. It's not really even intended as therapy.

Think of this book as a friend to talk things through with - but one who promises not to say "but you don't look autistic".

This book can also act as a kind of preparation for your assessment - to help get things clear in your head, and to direct your thoughts towards the most relevant things.

But not everyone needs, wants or has access to a diagnosis as an adult, for a number of reasons. And for many people, even once you've been through the system and got the official stamp of approval (or disapproval), the support stops there.

A diagnosis may be important for many reasons, but a diagnosis in itself won't give you all answers you need.

This workbook aims to fill the gap between the harsh clinical terms used in a diagnostic report and the reality of your lived experiences and memories, to guide you towards a more holistic and balanced view of yourself.

JOIN THE YO SAMDY SAM MAILING LIST

For those who are looking for news, community and support beyond the scope of this book, I have a free mailing list where I send out e-mails every time I publish a new video, as well as tips and tricks for autistic people, and news/updates on my other projects.

I would love it if you joined, it's totally free and you can unsubscribe at any time.

https://subscribepage.io/autisticworkbook

WHAT MAKES YOU THINK YOU MIGHT BE AUTISTIC?

I find that a lot of people struggle to know whether they are really autistic or not because autism is a bit of a strange concept to grasp.

A definition of autism is almost impossible to write because what is, at its core, a neurological difference, results in a wide variety of behaviours and experiences that vary wildly from person to person, and can present very differently.

Official definitions will make references to deficits, disorders and flaws, as if the neurotypical standard of communication is a shining beacon, and neurotypical people never have miscommunications.

I truly believe that autism from the outside is a very different beast to autism from the inside, and definitions of autism should be evolving based on what autistic people themselves say about the condition.

But back to you. You are here reading this so you clearly have an idea of what autism is, and you likely relate to what you've heard. But there's a big fuzzy mush between "I think I might be a bit autistic" and "I'm definitely autistic" and that's the area which we're going to clarify and make sense of here.

As it stands, even though autism is a "neurotype" (i.e. a type of neurological functioning), in order to be officially diagnosed as autistic, you need to be assessed by a psychologist. There is no brain scan for autism, although that would be cool.

This means that diagnosticians are still relying on behavioural indicators (and often self-reported ones).

The way that psychologists make sure they are diagnosing people according to the same criteria is by using a reference document* which has a list of criteria which you need to meet in order to qualify for diagnosis. These criteria are not perfect, and by no means comprehensive, but they do give a starting point.

For example, "sensory issues" only get a passing mention in the DSM, but these are often extremely important aspects of an autistic person's life.

The workbook is about to begin. Hooray! You made it through the waffle! The next few pages contain prompts inspired by the DSM criteria for autism diagnosis, but written in plain English. Try to fill them out as completely as you can, with examples wherever possible.

Don't forget there is a space for extra notes at the back if you suddenly find you have a lot to say!

* The DSM-5 is used by many countries, but several countries use the ICD-11, which has more or less the same criteria for diagnosis. Generally speaking, you will be diagnosed with Autism Spectrum Disorder, but some countries still use the (outdated) term Asperger's Syndrome. They are both autism.

IT'S TIME TO THINK ABOUT "THE SOCIAL STUFF"

Autism is, in a large way, defined by your comparative ability or style of social communication and interaction, when compared with the broader population.

While the term "disorder" is very loaded, and research shows that autistic people actually often communicate better with other autistic people, there are certainly a number of social differences that can make building relationships and friendships tricky, to say the least.

This can be painful to face - I know that for years I truly believed I was "good with people", when what I was really good at was: remembering personal details, pattern recognition, and trying really hard at relationships; all skills that allowed me to fake the appearance of social skills while still being dreadful at maintaining the relationships I was so desperate to build.

Be honest with yourself here.

What were your friendships like as a child and as an adult?

Did friendships or relationships ever end with you thinking "what just happened?"

Do you find it hard to maintain conversations or engage with others in an expected way? Do you monologue, or fail to grasp small talk?

Do you avoid eye contact, "fake" making eye contact, or force yourself to do it?

Do you feel like making facial expressions is a bit like acting out your emotions, and it doesn't come naturally?

Do you struggle to read body language and non-verbal communication, especially when someone's words don't match their behaviour?

Do you struggle to express the intended tone in your voice, or interpret the tone of others?

other behaviour
/activities

RESTRICTIVE, REPETITIVE PATTERNS OF BEHAVIOUR... HUH?

If, at some point, you've read the diagnosis criteria for autism (if not, it's worth a read for its extremely obtuse representation of basic everyday things), you might have come across a category titled "Restrictive and Repetitive Patterns of Behaviour".

I'm not sure whether it's an intentional choice to make autism sound so alien, but it's totally unnecessary and I'll attempt to explain what they mean here in somewhat plainer language.

Stereotyped or repetitive motor movements

This simply means stimming, which is shorthand for "self-stimulatory behaviours" and can range from commonly known autistic behaviours (head banging, rocking, hand flapping) to less well-known ones like cheek biting, finger tapping, vocal stimming, knuckle cracking, or really any movement that is done for regulation purposes, whether that is to regulate frustration, sensory overload, emotional discomfort or pain. They can also express joy or excitement.

You can stim with your hands, feet or any part of your body, using your voice ("vocal stimming") or with small objects or fidget toys.

It's important to note that stims can easily be mistaken for tics (and vice versa), so if you have Tourette's (or suspect you do) it may be worth exploring this further with a professional. Repetitive movements are also associated with ADHD so it's definitely a complicated area, and beyond the scope of this workbook.

Everyone - neurotypical or otherwise - stims

I can sometimes HEAR the eyes rolling when I describe my stims and they turn out to be "everyday things" that "everyone does". What separates out autistic stimming from your everyday garden variety stimming is:

- Frequency - do you stim every day?
- Timing - do you stim more during times of stress?
- Urgency - does suppression cause discomfort?
- Intention - do you (consciously or unconsciously) stim in order to self-regulate?

Do you stim? If so, how? What effect does it have on you?

Do you have fixed routines or THINGS THAT ABSOLUTELY MUST STAY THE SAME?

Do you have difficulties with transitions? This could be either in your daily life or large life transitions.

E.g. transitioning from home to work, starting university

How do you react when plans change unexpectedly? Can you give any examples of this?

"EXCESSIVELY CIRCUMSCRIBED OR PERSEVERATIVE INTERESTS"

And they say autistic people are rude!

Autistic Special Interests are rather pathologised by the diagnostic criteria, but they can be an incredible source of joy for autistic people.

Some people have just one so-called "special interest", other people have many different interests that come and go throughout their lifetime. They can be pretty mainstream or delightfully weird, but what makes them autistic "special interests", as opposed to simply "hobbies", is the intensity that from the outside often looks like obsession.

Is it unusual that a 10 year old girl growing up in the 90s loved the Spice Girls? Not at all!

Is it unusual that she memorised obscure information about them, cut out newspaper snippets and collected every magazine? That she wanted to talk about them all the time and listen to their music on repeat? Now THAT'S more like it!

INFODUMP TIME! Here is a safe space to write down all the things that you've been inexplicably and borderline obsessed with throughout your life...

SENSORY PROCESSING

Research suggests that as many as 90-95% of autistic people have sensory processing differences (the reverse, however, is not true).

Being hypo- or hyper-sensitive to sensory input is therefore often a key part of the autistic experience, that can heavily influence behaviour in all areas of life.

The next few pages are split into the different senses. You will likely have different experiences or sensitivities for each sense.

I highly recommend learning more about your own sensory profile (see resources section for book recommendations) as this can drastically improve your everyday quality of life.

For the next section, write down your preferences, sensitivities and any behaviours that you do to compensate (if relevant). I have provided a couple of examples in each category.

SMELL

E.g. obsessively sniffing things, getting overwhelmed by perfumes or strong detergent/chemical smells

TASTE

E.g. having a very limited palate, the need for crunchy things, avoiding certain textures, seeking stimulation through food

SIGHT

E.g. seeking out visual stimulation through fairy lights, wearing sunglasses to deal with light sensitivity, avoiding clothing with loud prints

HEARING

E.g. wearing headphones to block out noise, finding other tasks harder in a noisy environment, self-regulating by playing loud music, needing subtitles even without hearing loss

TOUCH

E.g. disliking being touched at all or in certain ways, liking to stroke soft fabrics or certain textures, difficulties with self-care tasks such as brushing teeth or showering due to the sensory input

VESTIBULAR
(balance/movement)

E.g. needing to rock or swing, enjoying sports that stimulate this sense like dance or gymnastics, having poor balance (or dyspraxia)

INTEROCEPTION (feeling sensations within the body)

E.g. being under-aware of the need to urinate, not noticing hunger cues, being over responsive to rises/drops in heart rate or blood sugar levels

PROPRIOCEPTION (locating the body in the world)

E.g. often bumping into things like tables or door frames, poor posture, bad at ball sports, clumsiness

LET'S TALK ABOUT YOUR CHILDHOOD...

Autism is considered a developmental condition, which means that it is present in childhood and will be continue to be present throughout your life.

Some things (like a traumatic brain injury) can cause symptoms that mimic autism, so asking about your childhood is one way for diagnosticians to check that there are no other explanations.

It is very common for late diagnosed autistic adults to compensate or "mask" their autism and only show traits later on as life becomes more complicated and stressful. For example, you might have found it relatively easy to navigate the social world of 7 year olds, but struggled when the social rules "changed" during adolescence. Or you might have got by with your coping mechanisms when you had your needs met as a child, but struggled when you had to live on your own, meet your own needs, and manage your own life.

Were all your traits present as a child? Did anything develop later? Did this coincide with any other events in your life?

imposter!

IMPOSTER SYNDROME

Imposter syndrome can be experienced in a variety of situations but in the context of an autism diagnosis it is likely to look like:

- Doubting yourself ("I can't really be autistic")
- Comparing yourself to others ("They have things so much worse than me")
- Thinking you might have tricked yourself or the person diagnosing you into believing you are autistic
- Finding it difficult to accept help

Almost everyone diagnosed as an adult experiences this from time to time

(Yes, even me!)

It can be very hard to deal with, especially when you have people around you who might ACTUALLY doubt you and reinforce these beliefs. Even if that person isn't in your life anymore, you may carry around their judgements as an internalised voice (especially when they come from parents or other authority figures).

Ultimately, to face imposter syndrome head on, what we need to break down are some of your core beliefs surrounding autism and disability.

Remember, there is no Oppression Olympics. We've all lived different lives, and you don't get judged for having it harder or easier than anyone else.

Not here anyway.

Autism is a spectrum, and what that means is that we all have a unique constellation of traits, strengths, and weaknesses. We might be very good at one thing, and very bad at another.

Thinking of someone as "more autistic" than you (or your loved one) because they have weaknesses in certain areas makes about as much sense as calling a chilli peanut "more peanuty" than a chocolate covered peanut.

What (or who) is the biggest trigger of your doubt/s? If it's a person, what do they say?

Do you have any beliefs about autism that pop into your head when you are experiencing imposter syndrome?

E.g. "If I was really autistic I would..."
"I can't be autistic because I can..."

Where did you get these beliefs about autism or autistic people? Do you think they are true?

Do you struggle with the idea of seeing yourself (or being seen) as disabled? Why?

What would happen if someone took away all your coping mechanisms? Do you think you would suddenly seem "more" autistic?

masking

MASKING

Masking is something that many autistic people do - especially those diagnosed in adulthood. There is a widespread belief that autistic people have no ability to self-reflect and therefore cannot mask but this is not supported by research.

Essentially, masking is about appearing "not autistic" to the outside world, and developing strategies to do so. It can be an unconscious or conscious act, and is usually deeply knitted into your personality by the time you get to adulthood.

It requires a great deal of energy and effort, and often leads to burnout, identity crises or mental health problems.

However, it can be a strategy that allows an autistic person to make and keep friends, find work, and otherwise live a "normal" life to an outside observer.

TYPES OF MASKING

Blending in: Dampening your autistic responses, maybe by stimming less obviously, or not at all.

Shallow compensation: Learning or developing rules or strategies which might help you in conversations, like memorising scripts for small talk, or basic "rules" for eye contact and greetings.

Deep compensation: Developing long term strategies for understanding people based on context. Allows you to "understand" people but this is from an intellectualised position that takes continued energy and does not happen naturally.

Accommodation: Changing your environment to help or disguise traits, for example by choosing a job that requires little social interaction, or moving to a different country, . This is often done subconsciously, and by those with more financial security.

Do you relate to the feeling of being a social chameleon? (Changing your personality according to the situation you are in)

Have you suppressed or adapted your stims to be more subtle over time?

Do you spend social situations in a state of hypervigilance (e.g. monitoring facial expressions or tone of voice) in order to keep up?

Do you mentally prepare or "script" things that you want to say during a future conversation?

Do you have memories of teaching yourself how to socialise? This might have been with the help of TV, film, books or by copying your peers.

Do you use strategies or techniques to help you in conversations that other people appear not to need?

Do you feel like you are putting on an act or a persona in most social situations? If so, how?

Do you compensate in any way for poor organisational and planning skills?

E.g. being an obsessive "list" person, sticking rigidly to plans, lying to teachers at school about late homework

Think about your sensory issues that we went through earlier. Have you "accommodated" yourself by buying particular things?

E.g. compression leggings, sunglasses, headphones, seamless socks

A NOTE ON UNMASKING

As soon as we learn about autistic masking, it can be tempting to think that the path to freedom simply involves "unmasking".

Unfortunately life is rarely that simple and this is no exception.

You may have built up these strategies over a number of years, probably as a means of survival, and in many cases it is sometimes hard to tell where the mask ends and where you begin.

My advice is to take things slowly, and experiment with leaving things behind which no longer serve you. It could be something simple, like seeing how it feels to be more relaxed about maintaining less eye contact in a conversation, instead of constantly monitoring yourself.

There's no rule book or time limit to unmasking, but when your strategies hurt you more than they help you, it may be time to reflect on this.

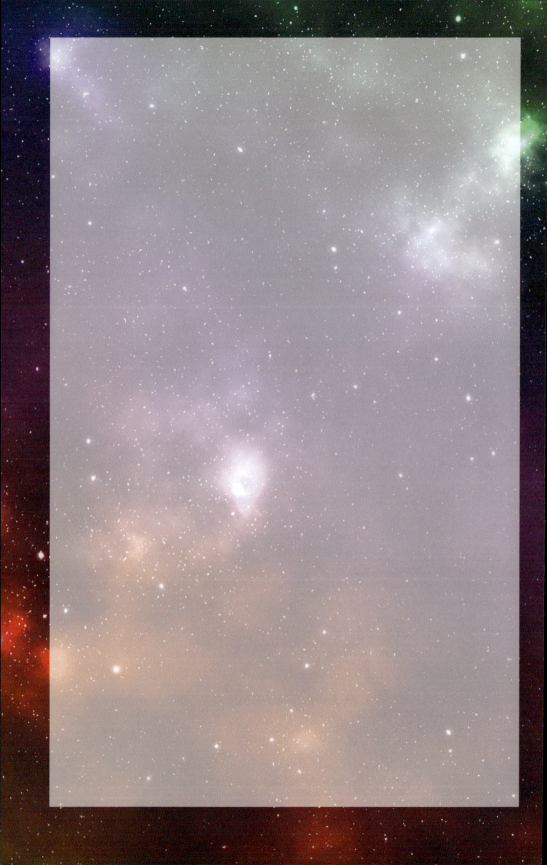

diagnosis

WILL AN AUTISM DIAGNOSIS BENEFIT YOU?

Maybe you're already on a waiting list. Maybe you've got no idea if you want a diagnosis or not. Maybe you've already been diagnosed (feel free to skip this section if so).

In many countries, an official diagnosis brings some support, in others you might be lucky with a pamphlet. Before making a decision, find out what you are entitled to.

A diagnosis is not a panacea and there are benefits and drawbacks to it, like with anything. These will vary greatly based on your personal situation.

Have a look at the pros and cons on the next page and see which ones are likely to be relevant to you. Please pay special attention to the last "con" - in many countries, you are not allowed to immigrate there with an autism diagnosis (unbelievable, but true) and a diagnosis could be used against you in legal settings.

POTENTIAL PROS

- External validation and confirmation
- Possible financial or social support available
- Accommodations from employers
- Your loved ones might take an official diagnosis more seriously

POTENTIAL CONS

- Stigma
- Little to no support in many areas of the world
- Possible discrimination from employers
- No guarantee that your loved ones will recognise or respect a diagnosis
- Potential legal issues (immigration, child custody)

What would a diagnosis mean to you?

What are the potential benefits to getting a diagnosis?

What are the potential drawbacks to getting a diagnosis?

Imagine some time in the future. A psychologist has declared you "officially autistic". How does that feel?

What do you plan to do after diagnosis? Shout it from the rooftops? Keep it private? Find support?

other identities

OTHER IDENTITIES

No person (autistic or otherwise) exists in a vacuum. We are all a messy mix of our other identities, which impact us in many different ways. Your autistic identity may interact with your identity as a parent, your sexuality, gender, race, class or additionally disability.

A lot of autistic people can belong to a few marginalised groups at once. For example, trans people are 3-6 times more likely to be autistic compared to cis (non-trans) people, and there is a link between autism and certain physical disabilities like epilepsy, hypermobility or gastro-intestinal issues, meaning that we are disproportionately likely to have additional health problems.

It's important to think about how your identities and privileges affect your autistic experience, as privileges in one area might conceal certain autistic traits, and disadvantages might intensify them.

For example:

If your parents could afford private school you might have had smaller classes at school and coped better overall because there was less noise and more personal attention.

If you had an atypical gender presentation you might have attracted more attention from peers at school, leaving you less able to "fly under the radar" with your other traits.

If you grew up in a country where you were considered "foreign" or in a racial or social minority, your neurological differences may have been attributed to cultural differences.

Autistic traits might have been missed or misattributed to an existing health condition or mental health diagnosis.

Living on a low income or unstable housing might lead to fewer options to accommodate yourself from a sensory perspective, leading to more frequent shutdowns or meltdowns.

What are some of your identities that are relevant to your experience of autism?

How do these identities impact your experience of autism and the world around you?

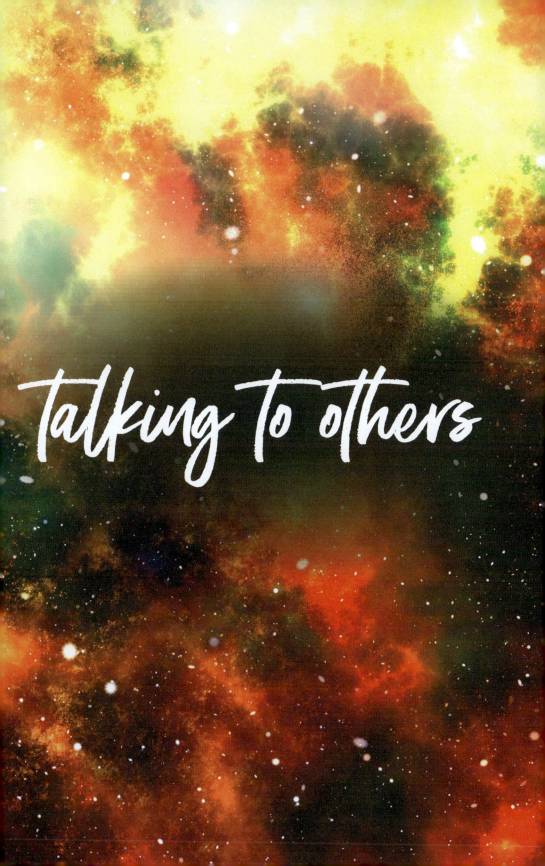

talking to others

There may come a time when you want to share some (or all) of this with your family or friends. This is understandably quite a daunting prospect, because, as it turns out, other people don't often care about the single most important revelation of our lives that explains absolutely everything about us. How rude!

People often ask me how to approach this topic with friends and family, as if I'll have some magical trick that will produce the desired result of acceptance and validation.

I don't (sorry!)

Ultimately the way they react has nothing to do with you. Some people will surprise you. Others may disappoint you.

But I would encourage you to give people time to learn and time to adjust. Point them in the direction of some easy to understand resources (see the end of this book for a few good ones).

My main advice for talking to people about autism is, try to get it clear before you start what you want to communicate. My original method, where I drank a bottle of wine and cried on my mother's lap for an hour, is not terribly effective and can be alarming for others (although "Sam's ill-advised coping mechanisms" would make a fun topic for my next book).

Maybe you want to assert firm boundaries and simply inform them that this is who you are?

Perhaps you want to point to examples from your childhood and show them how this matches up with the diagnostic criteria?

Maybe you want to tell them about masking and why this means that you don't "look autistic".

Use the next section to get it clear in your head what YOUR priorities are.

A NOTE ABOUT DISCLOSURE

Telling your family and friends is very different from disclosing your diagnosis in a more formal setting like a workplace.

There are legal implications to disclosing diagnosis in many countries, which could mean that employers are required to support you and make "reasonable adjustments" at work.

That definitely does not mean that you MUST disclose your diagnosis. Discrimination and stigma are still very much real and present, and unfortunately, you can never be sure of people's real opinions until they are put to the test.

Your manager might have an autistic 5-year old, and seem to "get it", but does that mean they are willing to put forward their autistic employee for that big promotion?

The decision to disclose your autism is of course up to you, but proceed with caution.

Who do you most want to share your diagnosis with? Why?

How much do they know about autism? Do you feel confident explaining concepts to them if they have questions?

Are you prepared for negative or dismissive reactions from others, and how do you plan to deal with them?

What are the top three things about autism and how it affects you that you most want to communicate to others?

1.

2.

3.

what now?!

WHAT NOW?! I HEAR YOU BELLOW

Congratulations on making it to the end of the workbook! You are probably exhausted, but I hope you have significantly more clarity in your life than when you began.

The journey of exploring your autistic identity is something that can last many years, and that's not taking into account those pesky waiting lists for diagnosis... which can also last for years.

If you had no trouble at all filling this workbook with relevant examples from your own life, this heavily suggests that you may be autistic, but of course it doesn't necessarily mean you are. I can't diagnose you through the page, but I would suggest using your new-found self-knowledge to investigate further.

This may be the end of the workbook, but it is far from the end of your journey.

RESOURCES

WEBSITES

Neuroclastic - a website/blog run entirely by autistic people - https://neuroclastic.com/

Embrace Autism - has several autism tests available to take for free - https://embrace-autism.com/

BOOKS

Unmasking Autism by Dr. Devon Price

Living Sensationally by Winnie Dunn

Life on the Autism Spectrum: A Guide for Girls and Women by Karen MacKibbin

Neurotribes: The Legacy of Autism and the Future of Neurodiversity by Steve Silberman

Spectrum Women: Walking to the Beat of Autism edited by Barb Cook & Dr Michelle Garnett.

The Reason I Jump: one boy's voice from the silence of autism by Naoki Higashida

We're Not Broken: Changing the Autism Conversation by Eric Garcia

Here are some useful terms commonly used to describe autistic and other neurodivergent experiences:

Alexithymia Subclinical inability to identify and describe your own emotions.

Autism (interchangeable with autism spectrum disorder and autism spectrum condition) A neurological condition characterised by differences and difficulties in socialising, communication, sensation and information processing.

Burnout A long-term response to stress which includes fatigue, reduced ability to deal with sensory stimuli, seeming "more autistic" and losing certain skills or coping mechanisms. Can often be mistaken for depression.

Dyscalculia A learning disability marked by difficulties with maths, number-related content and working memory for numbers.

Dyslexia A learning disability involving difficulties with reading, writing, and spelling, as well as other visual information processing, such as interpreting maps.

Dyspraxia A lifelong condition which impacts someone's ability to coordinate movement, and affects gross motor skills. It can often be perceived as 'clumsiness'.

Executive functioning A set of cognitive processes that are necessary for the cognitive control of behaviour. They include; self-awareness, inhibition, non-verbal working memory, verbal working memory, emotional self-regulation, planning, and problem solving.

Interoception A sense that helps us to understand what is going on inside our bodies, for example the feeling of fullness, thirst, heat, or cold.

Masking A sort of social "camouflage" that some autistic people develop and use in order to meet social expectations. In addition to making the person appear "less autistic", it may also conceal the person's need for support and discourage authentic expression of self, leading to long-term psychological and self-esteem issues.

Meltdown An intense response to overwhelming situations characterised by the loss of behavioural control. This can be expressed verbally or physically, and is not deliberate or intentional. A meltdown can often be followed by feelings of shame, regret, and fear.

Neurodiversity The range of differences in individual brain function and behavioural traits, regarded as part of normal variation in the human population. Coined in 1998 by Australian sociologist Judy Singer.

Neurodivergent Diverging from the neurological norm. Can be used as a "catch all" term for a variety of mental and neurological conditions. It is NOT a synonym for autism.

Neurotypical Not displaying or characterized by autistic or other neurologically atypical patterns of thought, behaviour, or brain function.

Overwhelm Sensory overwhelm can happen when the input of information from your senses feels like too much. This might build up gradually or suddenly and can increase the likelihood of meltdowns or shutdowns in the near future.

Proprioception Perception or awareness of the position and movement of the body, and the sense of one's own limbs in space.

Selective/situational mutism An anxiety disorder where a person is unable to speak in certain social situations, such as with classmates at school or relatives they see infrequently. This is different from apraxia of speech, which affects many non-speaking autistic people, but has a different root cause.

Sensory processing disorder (SPD) A neurological disorder which causes challenges with processing, taking in, or responding to sensory information. 90-95% of autistic people also have SPD.

Shutdown A muting response to extreme stress or overwhelm. The person may be unable to speak, carry out basic tasks or instructions, and may not move or respond.

Special interest This refers to the often intense passions that many autistic people have. This could be in one or multiple areas, and can be directed at any topic imaginable.

Stimming Self-stimulatory behaviour which is typically characterised by repetitive physical movements, sounds, words, or fiddling with objects.

notes

Printed in Great Britain
by Amazon

43412230R00064